AF254648

Published by Suzo Media
Book design by Chryss Yost

ISBN-13: 978-1-7350460-0-6

www.susanreadcronin.com

NOTICES

Poems & Art
by
Susan Read Cronin

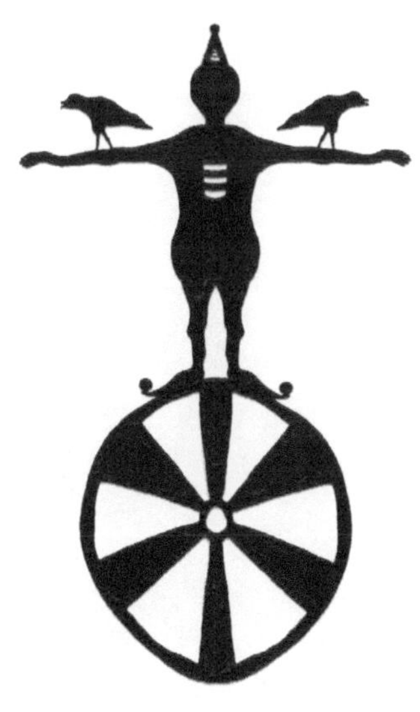

SUZO MEDIA, SANTA BARBARA
2020

ART

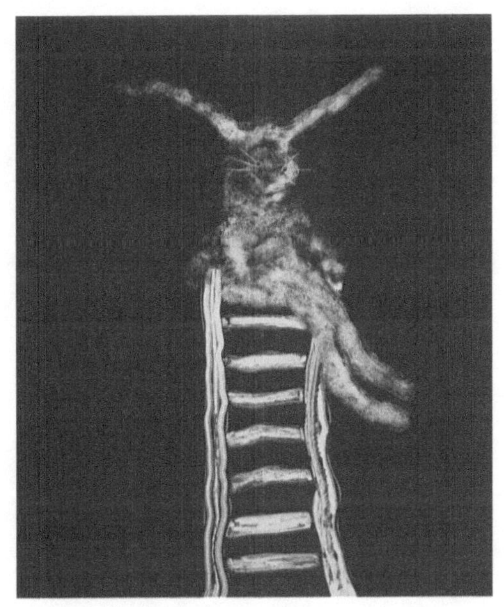

For Ted

SECOND-BORN DAUGHTERS

Maybe I am one of those
Chinese daughters:
the second girl born live—only
one child was meant to thrive.

One of those Chinese daughters
whose mouth was filled
with sand or put up
for adoption in some foreign land.

A daughter
laid down on a corner,
wrapped in blue cloth,
brought home by a stranger,
suckled on fish broth.

Maybe she and I, being
those second born daughters,
those second-hand daughters,
those castoff girls,

maybe we both speak
that secret language,
the language where a word goes
missing every night,
abandoning
its shadow
in the morning light.

TUCKER LESLIE'S 6TH BIRTHDAY PARTY—
SUMMER OF 1959

Be sure to say Please and Thank You. Don't play
with any of the presents. When it's time
to go, thank Mrs. Leslie, curtsey,
shake her
hand and look her in the eye.

Armed with these instructions and the present
I had to pick out for the girl
I don't know,
I am dropped off at the front door
of a large modern concrete house—
the home of Tucker Leslie: a pile of kids

I don't know,
Pin-the-Tail-
on-the-Donkey, Woody Woodpecker
cartoons, creamed chicken,
rice and canned peas, pink
sponge cake, seven candles—
One to grow on,
Make a wish!
blown out.

My lace collar itches me.
Crap! I think, *Crap!*
although I don't know that word yet.
Is it Tucker Leslie or
           Leslie Tucker?

Time to open presents—Will Leslie
like my gift? I can't
tell. I don't
care.
I am too focused on my upcoming *good-bye*—

Is it *Mrs. Leslie or*
     Mrs. Tucker?
My underpants ride up.

I hear my mother call my name.
The birthday girl's mother stands by her
at the front door.

I look her in the eye,
shake
her hand, curtsey—
Thank you so much for inviting me
to Leslie's party, Mrs. Tucker.
I had a wonderful time.

In the car, my mother corrects me—
It is Mrs. Leslie NOT
               Mrs. Tucker.
The girl's name is Tucker.

I say nothing,
snuffle,
look down
       at my shoes,
               pearl button, eyelet strap.

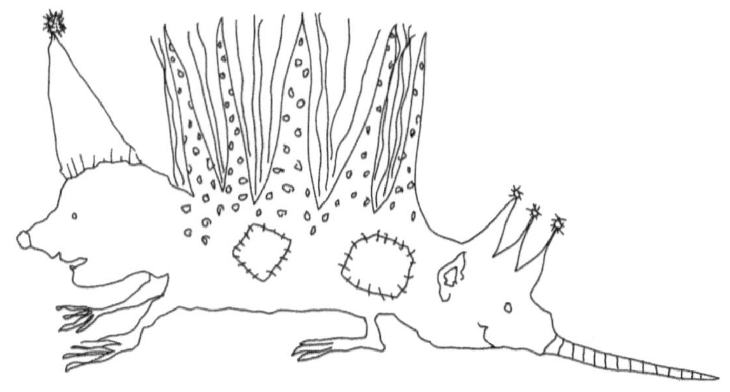

INVERSE UNIVERSE

I may not be able
to control
the weather outside,
but I can
control the atmosphere inside my head—

Cranium-contained
limitless inverse universe.

MARRIAGE METAPHORS

Monogrammed wedding present—
a set of blue terry towels.

Why my maiden name initials? I ask
my aunt—twice-married.
Her reply, *Trust me—*
Your towels will long outlive your marriage.

The first ten years of wedded bliss,
those towels, thick and thirsty,
lick the moisture from taut breasts
and backs, swaddle children after baths.

At twenty years of married life,
they fade to dingy grey.
Their edges fray
where the cat has snagged its claws.
They sop up rains
that breach the windows left

                     open

by mistake.

After thirty year of knotted ties,
things change for them—
tired infidels—
turned into tatters,
torn into squares—
rags,
they lie
lifeless in a pile
            under the sink.

After forty years—
those terry shreds
shrivel and shrink.
And falling

                              apart,
they limp their way
out
to the trash.

What made me keep them for so long?
Maybe to prove
to my aunt—
she was wrong.

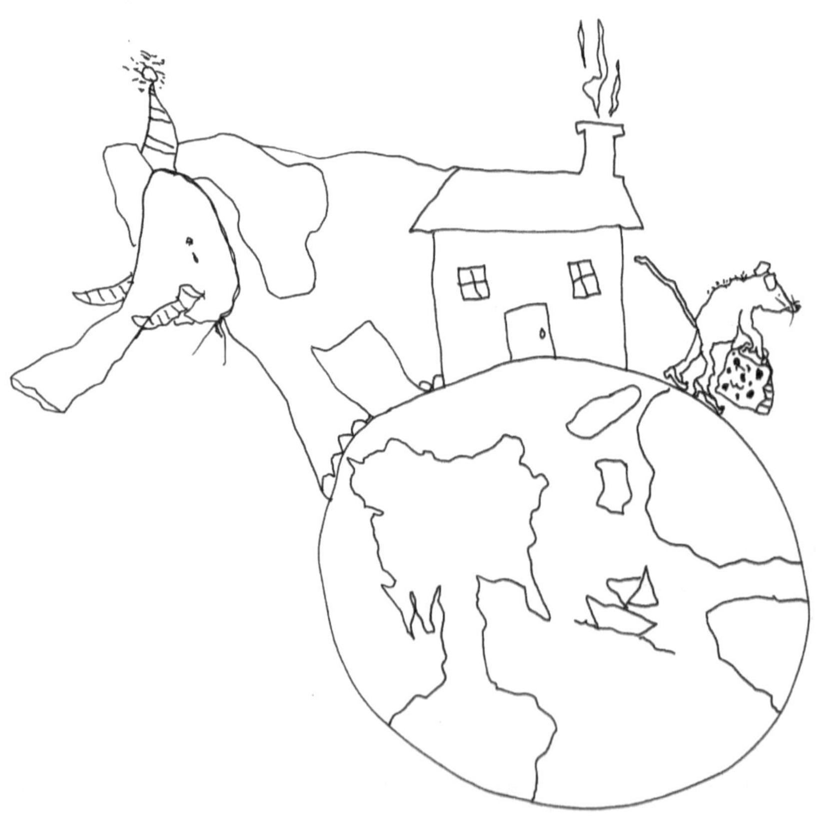

ALL THE THINGS I WOULD HAVE BOUGHT AT THE STORE I CAN'T REMEMBER THE NAME OF

I can remember the names of all the girls
in my shack at the camp I went to each summer.

On the Fourth of July, we marched
in the town parade
in our starched green jumpers,
middy shirts, saddle shoes.

In rows of ten across, we followed
the horse brigade and fought the flies
swarming their flanks.

We high-stepped and sidestepped
around steaming piles of horse shit
and pockets of pothole tar.

Our reward at the end of the route was a stop
at the store I can't
remember the name of—
the store that was part hardware, part
sundry, part penny candy palace.

The smell of its oiled floors, wavy with age,
assaulted our senses. We barged through the door,
drinking in the cool dark air
laced with grease,
newsprint, and cardboard. Chocolate.

A quarter was all I had. It felt hot in my hand.
It was enough—to visit the candy counter, to wait
my turn to fill a brown paper bag

with a pair of red wax lips, a pack of spruce gum—
Oh! that subtle taste of resinous wood shavings—
some chocolate mints, and three strips of sugar
dot candy—those narrow slips of paper
with columns of glued-on pastel circles of sugar
to be nibbled, sucked, or bitten off
by girls who'd been living in the woods for weeks.

If I had had more money, what would I have bought
at the store I can't remember the name of?

No doubt. More candy.

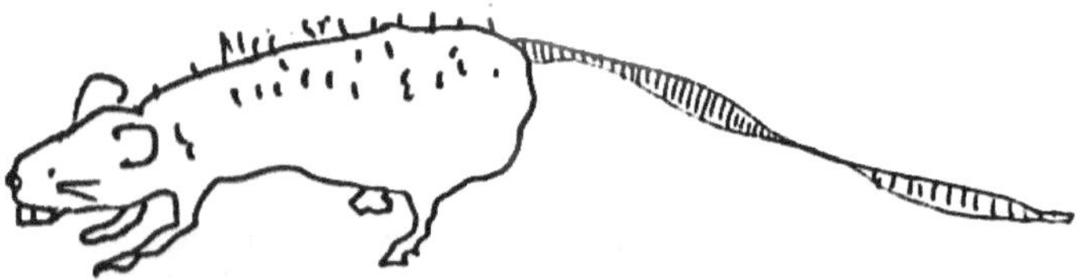

FOR MY FATHER ON HIS 75ᵀᴴ BIRTHDAY

Your first birthday party I remember,
you were turning thirty. I was five.

A gorilla pushed people into the pool.
Wet tracks sopped the shaggy rug
as guests went upstairs for a change of clothes.
A boozy-breathed man pressed a quarter in my hand.
I had died and gone to heaven—
rich beyond measure.

When I inhaled that lime green sour ball years later,
remember?
You held me upside down over the wastepaper basket.
I gagged, the ball
dropped,
plunk
        in the metal bin.
How strong you were!

I breathed in all you had to teach me—
how to:
drive a stick shift,
change a tire,
use sign language.
How you
welcomed silence,
laughed at bad luck,
loved your children.

You're seventy-five now.
I'm fifty, a quarter behind you,

yet finding myself rich—
beyond measure.

SOMETHING TO GET EXCITED ABOUT

I feel sorry for her
                 having to hear
of her husband's latest affair
                 in a poem
he chooses to share
with thousands of people
                 on air—
                 on public radio—

We all hear how
someone else's
thighs blanket him in bed in some Paris hotel
and how he and this lover,
                 or perhaps another,
share not one, but two
bottles of wine, before stepping
out to dine on oysters and caviar.

Back at home,
              alone,
the famous poet's wife opens
a can of soup—
tomato bisque,
the kind seasoned with fresh basil.

Now this could be something
to get excited about.

A CHANGE OF TEETH

Your old teeth, I mourn their loss.
They were part of what attracted me
to you in the first place.

It was that snaggle tooth,
and one black tooth,
and those coffee stained nubbins
forming that crooked chorus line
that danced beneath your smile.
I loved the way you pulled your upper lip
over them, like a curtain.

You were embarrassed by them.
I loved them.

Then, when you had the money,
and lots of it,
you decided to fix them.
We could have bought
a car, or a condo,
but you wanted
new teeth to garage in your old mouth.

Pleased with the results you say,
This dentist is an artist–
I think he got them
just right.

Very nice! I say aloud–
all the while thinking,
But they're not you.

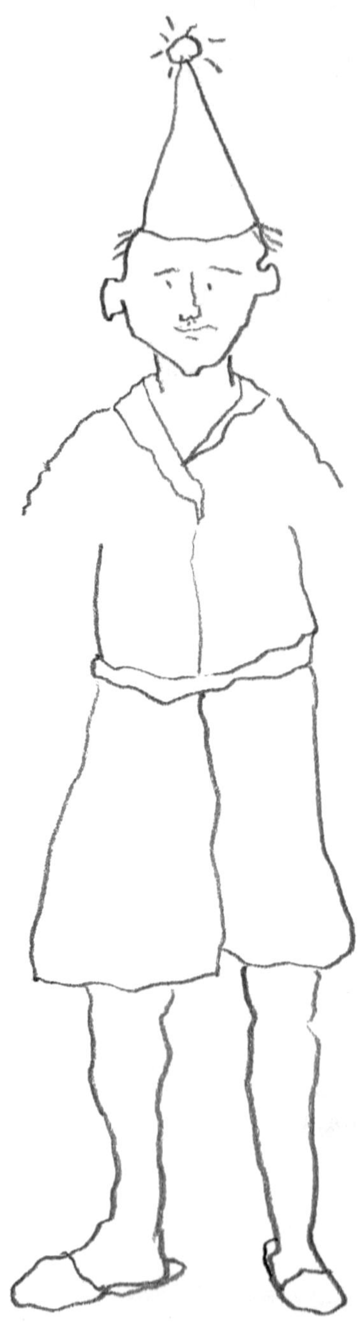

AT MIDNIGHT, SMELLING TOAST,
I COME DOWNSTAIRS TO FIND YOU
AT THE KITCHEN TABLE

There you are sipping Port
in the Windsor chair,
the piece of toast in your right hand,
tweed coat,
pocket square,
no pants,
only underwear.
Your bare feet sweep
the kitchen floor.
In the doorway,
I stand and grin
at this businessman,
little boy,
dear,
dear to me.

FILET OF SOLE

We've landed a table for two.
It's Valentine's Day
Chez Citronelle,
overlooking the North Sea.

The waiter's tie
is screened
with Klimt's *Kiss*.

A trio of courses appears
in slow succession:
lobster bisque,
filet of sole,
chocolate soufflé.

Three tables over,
a dark-haired man—mmm—
takes off his shoes.

So do I—

as the waiter hands me a long-
stemmed rose
and husband
        the bill.

1:42 PM AMTRAK SURFLINER

An old man stops by our table
of eight women. We're having
lunch at Pam's club.

He greets Pam,
then closes in behind her.
Resting his hands on her shoulders,
he smiles and swivels his head.

He takes us all in—
My! What a lovely group of gals you are!

Seven pairs of eyebrows
rise, tweezed unison,
wonder, *Who is this guy?*

Pam can't see him. She freezes
under the weight of him, pushing down on her shoulders.

He leaves.

She leans in, *That's Bob.*
He was sitting here, a month ago
waiting for his wife to meet him.
She never came.
She was that woman,
who was hit by the train.
Remember?
That was his wife.

At dessert, Bob pauses at our table again, with an Asian woman,
could have been his daughter.
He puts his arm around her waist:
This is Su Lin, from Taiwan and a journalist.

We all smile at her.

They walk away—
with light steps—
steps of lovers
newly in love.

In the distance I can hear the train coming.

ODE TO ATTRACTIVE MEN EVERYWHERE

Does he sleep in clean underwear,
or maybe in a ratty shirt?

Does he think it rude for you
to wonder what he wears to bed?

You do know one thing—
and he might think you rude, no matter.

When he sleeps in your dreams,
he sleeps in the nude.

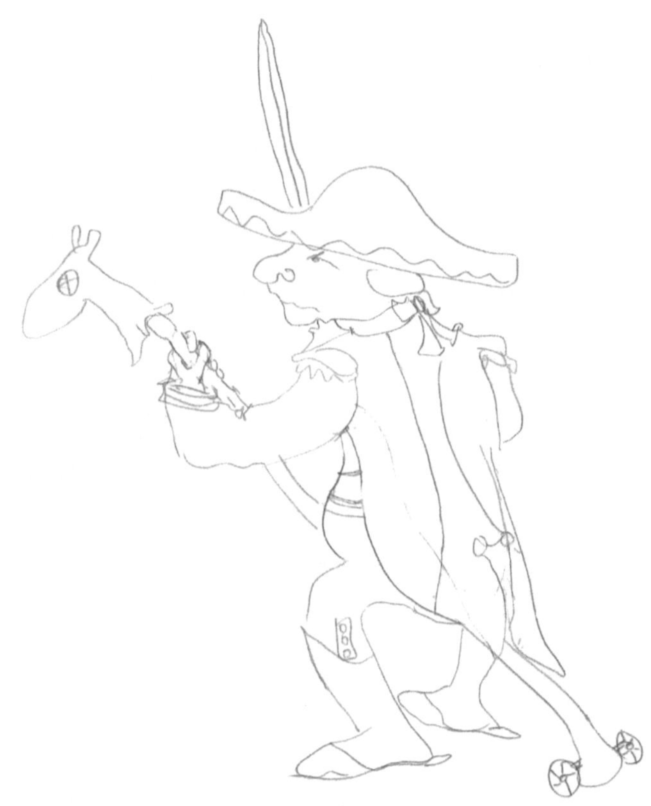

What Was It About Summer Camp

       that made me want to pack in April?
That made me ready to go
long before it was time to be away
for two months
in the New Hampshire woods?

Was it the slam of screen doors echoing
across the lake? The aluminum
pitchers filled with bright red bug juice?
The soft white bread, smeared
with butter and sugar?

Maybe it was the smell of frogs
in the inch of murk at the water's edge?
Or the overnight canoe trips,
sleeping under Orion?
Was it none of these—

Was it because
I had found my tribe,
uncovered that part of me
missing at home? I was
noticed—at last.

THE INCHWORM

Hanging by a thread
    that's how I find you.

You light upon my shoulder.
    I will carry you farther

than you've ever been before.
    I will take you up a trail

lined with bougainvillea.
    Your eyes will not see

the beauty spread before us—
    they will only sense
light and dark. You will turn into a moth.

Attracted by the light, in the dark
    you will fly into a flame

and bring with you no memory
of what you are now:

a small green stripe, stretching out
    to become a full inch

in the immeasurable world
    that lies—vast
        beyond my shoulder.

A QUEEN BEE'S FANTASY

Sometimes she lays spread eagle on a round table,
slowly pulling a mouchoir across her face—

Primping all day—a wildflower in the wind—
she waves about attracting her pollen-laden minions.

Or so she'd like to imagine.

The truth is, she is so busy laying eggs,
her head spins. She can't see straight.

Buried in some waxy shaft,
she wonders, *Do the drones even know who I am?*

THE JADE PLANT

It started out small when you left.
I watched it grow like you.

Sometimes, I would wash its chubby leaves
the same way I would wash your little hands.

And water it, then ignore it, intermittently.
Did I do the same to you?

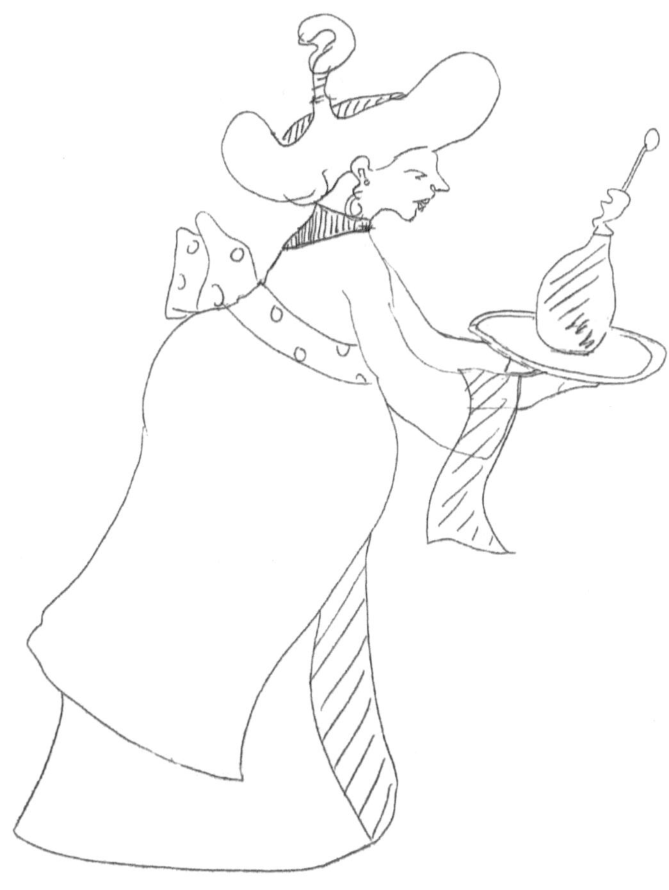

FATHER-IN-LAW

You dreamt your dad died.
Strange, you said.
He died a few years ago.

Remember how he used to say *po day do* for *potato?*
Remember his eight-foot high blueberry bushes?
His thick white hair? That shock!
How everyone at the funeral spoke of his wide hands?

He had laid down tracks inside all of us.

When you heard the train come through last night,
you climbed aboard if only for a short while.

THE STORY OF O

Her name was O.
She could never
remember names
so, she called everyone
Dearie.

She had three daughters:
Echo,
Ditto,
and
Freeto.

She was my mother's best friend—
they both developed
dementia,
or Alzheimer's,
or
whatever you call it.

Then they forgot

each other.

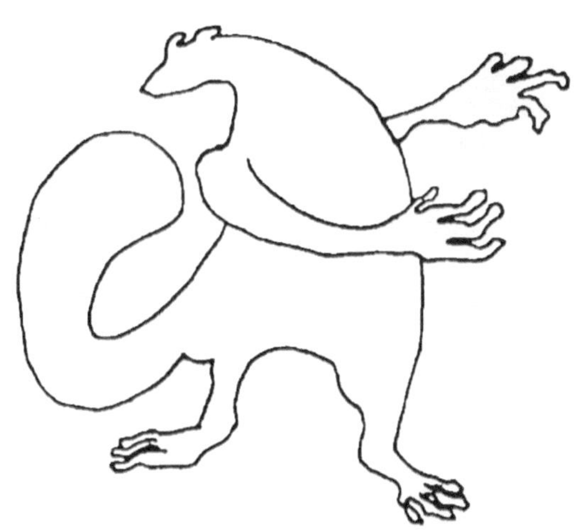

RELIQUARY FOR A BEST FRIEND

You keep her in your phone,
in your contacts list.

On her birthday each year,
your phone reminds you:

her name over a present icon,
white box, red bow.

Every day, you see her face
in your photo scroll.

She's in there. Smiles,
should I let my hair go gray?

Yes! Yes! you say.
You want to grow old with her.

But, no—
No—

The Drawer

     is full of them:
rosaries,
bottles full of pills.

The rosaries—one, a modest
knot of balls held together
with twine. A pressed tin crucifix
dangles off its end.
One, a string of glossy fat beads
blessed by the Pope himself.
One, a bulge in a vinyl pouch
closed in by a tiny shiny snap.

The pills—
long red caplets,
small orange tablets,
snowy little pillows,
some to make you bigger,
some to make you smaller,
some to make you disappear altogether.

More pills scatter loosely
on the blue liner—
vessels waiting to sink
in the river Styx,

unstrung rosaries,
unmoored pills,
sleep next to death,
deaf to the prayers
Dear God,
Oh! For a quick fix.

OH, SWEET LETHE

The operation was a success
or so I gather.

And during that forgotten time,
what was said? How many people
touched me? Did I lose my virginity?
Did they get right to work or dilly dally?

Did they careen around the room
waving knives, *look at me!?*
Did they laugh behind my back
or leave tracks— sponges, other spoor?

Was there a crowd in the amphitheater:
voyeurs, interns, priests?

Did I make myself a fool?
Or just lie there
     motionless,
     in a silent
     pool of
     drool?

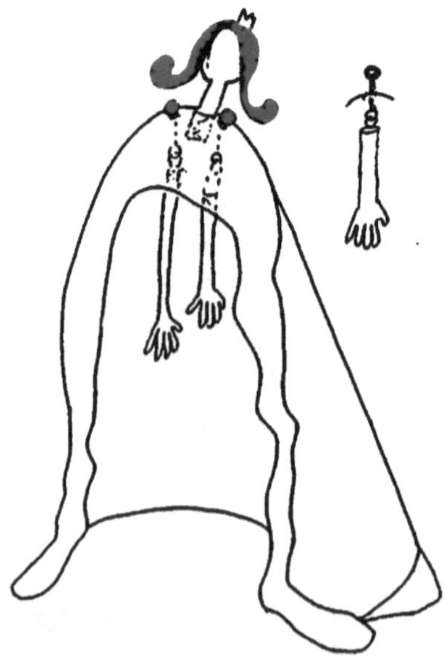

A LIFE CUT SHORT

I got the news
this morning.
My brother-in-law died
last night.

I call his wife.
I'm so sorry, I say.
She has people there,
so I keep it short.

I call his brother,
who says,
I called my brother
every day
before he died,
just to check in on him.

Now his nephew
is on the other line—
so, I cut it short.

I call his sister.
No answer—
I tell the silence—
I'm so sad, so sorry.

She calls right back.
I'm going to go
to the nurses' station
to let them have it.
Her Irish blood boils.
Blacken all their eyes.
He shouldn't have died.

Too soon.
They sent him
home too soon.
She needs to call
her daughters.
I make it short.

I call my husband's office.
He's busy now.

Your brother is dead.

He needs keep it short.
He's too busy to talk
right now.

I'm so sorry,
I say.

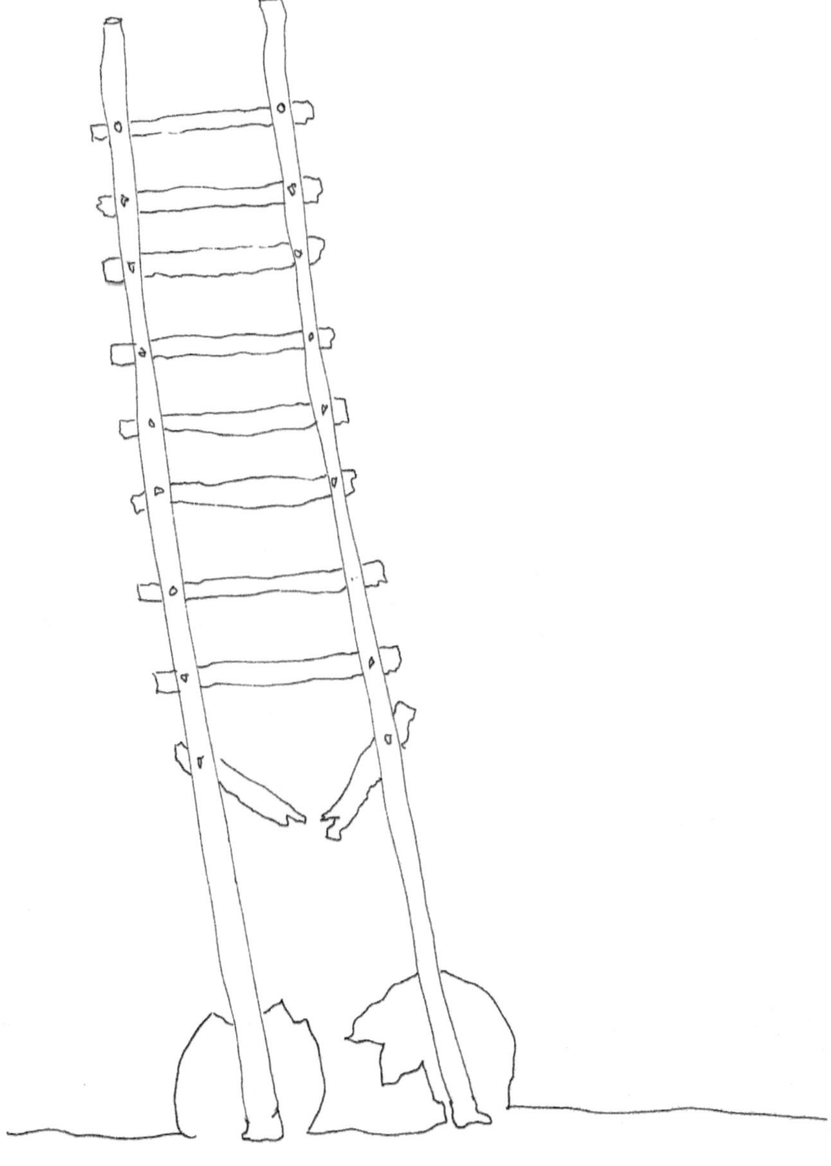

IF DEATH WERE ON MY DOORSTEP

If Death were on my doorstep,
would I let him in?

Or run like Hell?!

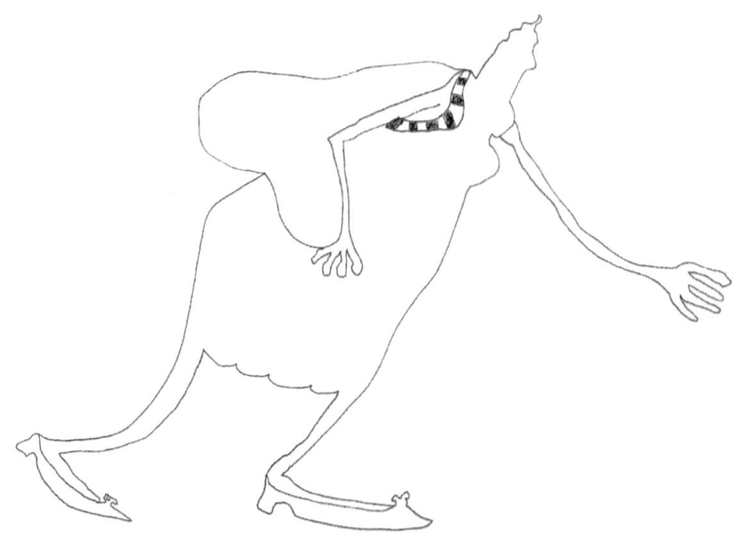

TEENAGE TRAVAILS WITH MY MOTHER

Excuse me, Ma'am,
says the Denver airport gift shop girl.
Please allow me to help you with that.

My mother helps herself,
pulls apart the display of silver bracelets
off the black velour bolster
on the glass-topped counter.

Hopi? Navajo?
I want them all!

The shop girl's eyes widen.
My mother squeals with delight,
thrusts all ten bracelets
at the girl.

Shall I wrap them for you, Ma'am?

My feet freeze in place
at the entrance of the store—
my red-cheeked fourteen-year old self
scuttles to an imaginary spot
far away—

I don't know this person,
I say to no one in particular.

A voice on the PA system calls our flight.

My mother tugs at
a carved wooden wolf
on a leather thong—
slips it over her head,

dances to the mirror.
I'll take this, too!
Her arm brushes a bowl
of smudge sticks.
Sage perfumes the air.

In the mirror,
her one good eye
catches a turtle shell rattle.
She robs it from its cradle,
shakes it with rhythmic wrist action.

Spell-bound, the shop girl watches
my mother skip,
one knee up high, then the other,
rocking back and forth
down the aisle of the airport gift store—

Ooooo wawawa! Ooooo wawawa!

The minute hand on my watch
spins around its face,
moving time ahead
at the speed of light.

Our flight is called again.
It's boarding.
        My stomach churns.
I yearn to run at break-neck speed
down the long polished hallway
to the gate.

Then I remember—
my mother has my ticket.

DANDELION OF PLYMOUTH ROCK

We came over together
on the Mayflower

the dandelion and I.

Kindred spirits,
both blonde,

now blanching,
full-sphere white crowns—

that ride the wind
instead of the waves,

our hair-like parachutes
in search of a moss-covered rock
on which to land.

HAIR

Most men your age are Friar Tucks
with straggly scraps pasted to their heads.

You love your hair.
And you loved your mother
more than you can say.

I can see it—

A manila file
marked with her name.
In it rests tissue paper
tucked around a lock of hair.

It was summer
when we strewed her ashes,
tossed roses on the water,
as the tide took her out,

her only marker now a grey wave,
buried deep in a file cabinet.

AFTER BEING TOGETHER FOR FORTY YEARS

Are you my affliction
or am I my own?
After all, aren't we
all part of one another?

The things I dislike in you
so much a part of me?

And vice versa, of course.

In a tsunami
you would have grabbed onto a tree,
floated to safety.

I would have gone down under. Gladly.

Not drowning in some old folks' home
having someone else wipe for me,
I would have been:
A hero!
Young...
Vibrant!
In her prime!
What a waste!

You would have liked
young women bringing casseroles
to our house.

WHEN

What year will it be
when
everything in my mailbox is marked
like me, *Return to Sender?*

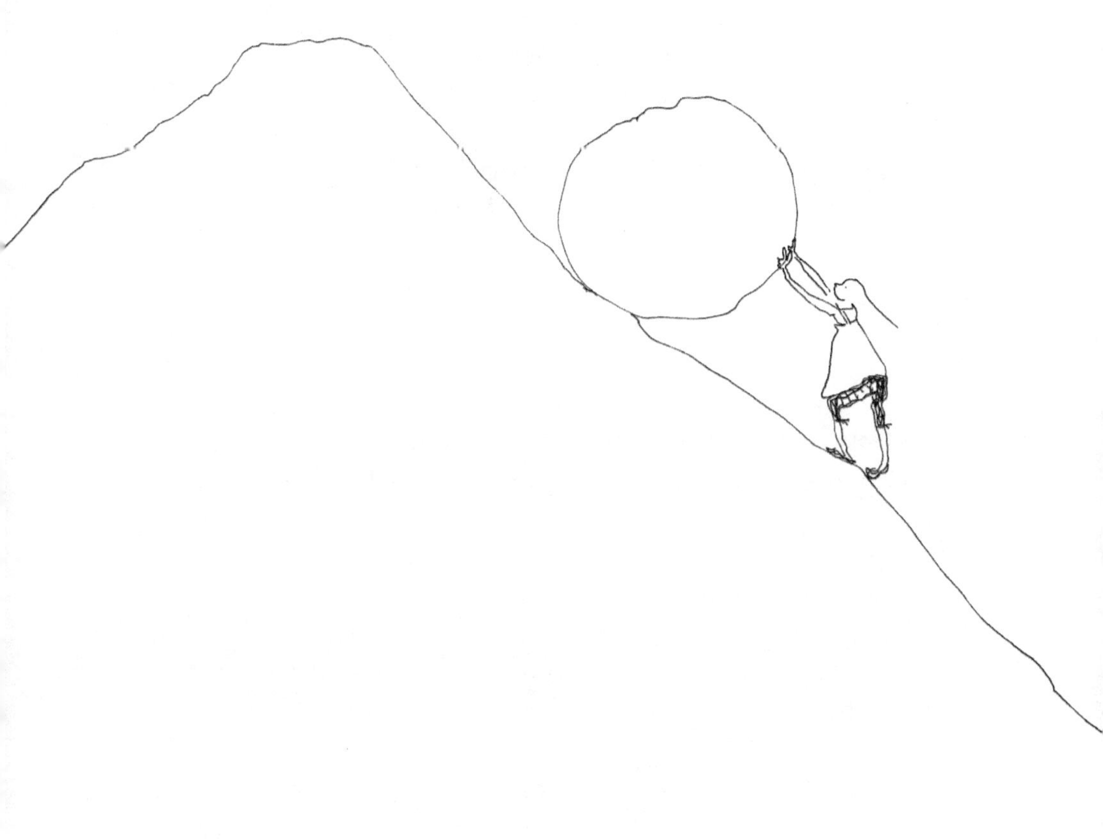

NOTES

In case you were wondering:

I always liked Hoss the best on Bonanza.
George was my favorite Beatle.
In fifth grade, I loved the Yankees.

I never saw hide nor hair of Tucker Leslie
after that birthday party. Maybe her name
really was Leslie Tucker?

The name of the Greek spirit of oblivion and
forgetfulness "Lethe" is pronounced *Leethee*.

O's third daughter was not named "Freeto."
Apologies.

My forebearers came on the Mayflower and I
am a Daughter of the American Revolution.
I went to one meeting and ate all three Jello salads.

I was brought up Catholic and haven't been
to mass or confession in years. Maybe
that's why I've taken up writing poetry.

Forgive me.

ACKNOWLEDGEMENTS

I wish to thank my friends and family for providing love, support, encouragement and some of the fodder for these works. The people listed below have my sincerest gratitude:

My husband Ted Cronin; my son Read Cronin and his daughter Teddy; my son Wright Cronin, his wife Rebecca, and their children Misha and Saffron;

Laure-Anne Bosselaar—What fun it is to work with you! Thank you for the laughter, wit, line-breaks, and use of your powder room. Tempus fugits around you;

dear friends, who leant their ears; and my tribe of amazing and talented relatives too numerous to list;

and for all the people I cannot remember,
thank you.

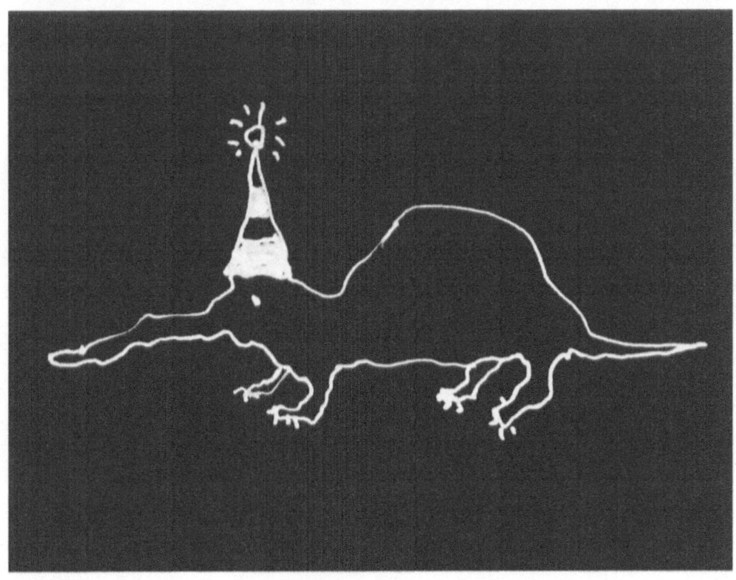

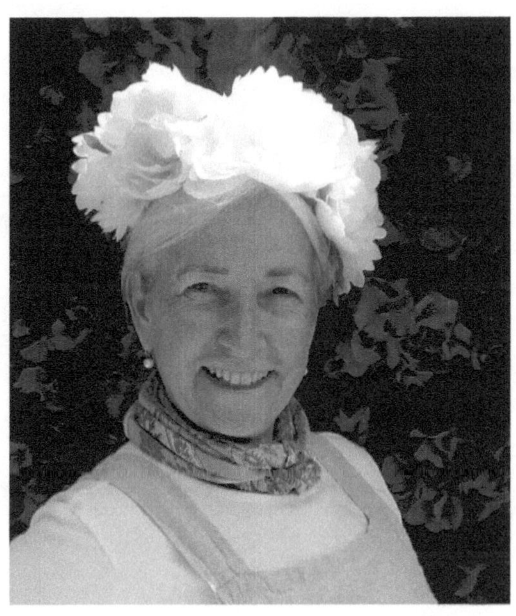

ABOUT THE AUTHOR

Susan Read Cronin was born with a silver spoon in her
mouth and moved on to a full set of steel braces. After completion
of successful orthodontia and three years at
The Madeira School, she went on to complete a degree in English at
Williams College.

During her extensive lifetime she has been a designer and
mail-order purveyor of *Suzo* costumes for children; a
bronze casting sculptor and, more recently,
an avid schnippenschearer.

She has under her belt few books of renown, including:
The Suzo Cut-a-logue
Bronze Casting in a Nutshell
The Magician's Assistant

This is her first book of poetry.